MASTER MACBOOK KEYBOARD HOTKEYS

Operate the Computer Seamlessly & Efficiently

MOMOH S.O

ISBN: 9798880177639

CONTENTS

PREFACE

In a fast-paced digital world of increasing computerization and digitization in every sector of the society.From the use of computers in schools for learning,hospitals,laboratories,financial markets,law enforcement,security and E-commerce,trades,government,
banks & financial organizations,
Agriculture,genetics,Engineering,biotechnology,sports & gaming to use in businesses and the corporate world.
The use of computer to carry out tasks and operations has become a common place.This coupled with great resignation,workers going remote and increasing work from home and the explosion in the adoption of freelancing and the sprouting up of various side hustles and gigs that can be

done remotely and require the use of the computer,from writing,to proof-reading & editing,publication,coding & programming,web & software development to graphic design and so on. To stand out in this fiercely competitive spaces and deliver or complete jobs utmost efficiency,a proficiency in the use of computer is imperative,if one ever hopes to stand out.

One the first approach to getting started,is to master and become proficient in the use of the computer hot keys and short cut keys.As they help to optimize one's working speed and efficiency.

This book puts together all the Macbook computer hot keys and keyboard shortcut key combinations for various operations around the computer.From use in writing and Doc word documents,general key board hot keys,to use in the image application,File explorer and to use in the Macbook safari browser applications and other advance applications to help make operations seamless,fast and efficient.

ABOUT THE AUTHOR

The Author Momoh S.O is a learned & well-read writer,a programmer,web-developer, with a B.Sc in Computer engineering & technology With an advanced knowledge in proof-reading,typing,editing,web technology and web app developments and vast in a wide array of programming language such as;

HTML,CSS,PHP and JAVASCRIPT.He has worked with various models and brands of computers,keyboard types and keypads from the Microsoft windows,PDAs to the macintosh and Macbook computers.

TABLE OF CONTENT

SUMMARY

In a fast-paced digital world of increasing computerization and digitization in every sector of the society.From the use of computers in schools for learning,hospitals,laboratories,financial markets,law enforcement,security and E-commerce,trades,government,
banks & financial organizations, Agriculture,genetics,Engineering,biotechnology,sports & gaming to use in businesses and the corporate world.
The use of computer to carry out tasks and operations has become a common place.This coupled with great resignation,workers going remote and increasing work from home and the explosion in the adoption of freelancing and the sprouting up of various

side hustles and gigs that can be done remotely and require the use of the computer,from writing,to proof-reading & editing,publication,coding & programming,web & software development to graphic design and so on. To stand out in this fiercely competitive spaces and deliver or complete jobs utmost efficiency,a proficiency in the use of computer is imperative,if one ever hopes to stand out.

One the first approach to getting started,is to master and become proficient in the use of the computer hot keys and short cut keys.As they help to optimize one's working speed and efficiency.

This book puts together all the Macbook computer hot keys and keyboard shortcut key combinations for various operations around the computer.From use in writing and Doc word documents,general key board hot keys,to use in the image application,File explorer and to use in the

Macbook safari browser applications and other advance applications to help make operations seamless,fast and efficient.

INTRODUCTION

In the previous book *COMPUTER HOT KEY MASTERY* in this series,we looked at all the computer shortcut and hotkeys for the windows operating system computer keyboards and how to apply them.In this book,we will delve into the macintosh(Macbook) computer keyboard hotkeys and upon completion,the reader will become proficient and can expertly operate on any Macbook keyboard seamlessly without any glitch,hitch or hassle .

In this book,we will examine key areas and application software that

commonly employ the use of keyboard and the shortcut key combinations,the functions associated with them and how to apply them.The following areas will be considered;

> ➢ **General Keyboard short cuts**
> ➢ **Photos Application**
> ➢ **Safari Browser**
> ➢ **Document(Docs,pptx,Spread sheet,etc) Hot keys**
> ➢ **Power Keys Short Cuts**
> ➢ **Finder(File Explorer) Hotkeys,etc**

Before we get started,lets take a quick look at some function key

comparison between the windows keyboard and the Macbook keyboards.

● **In the windows keyboard**
The control key is represented as Ctrl.
In the Macbook keyboard however,it is represented by the key ⌃

● **The Alternate key(alt) is represented by the(Option key)**

- The Cap lock key is represented by the key 🔼

- An important function key in the Macbook keyboard,is the Command key(⌘) which is has the function of any of the Ctrl key or the windows logo key on windows computer keyboard.

Dive in to the world of Macbook hotkeys!

GENERAL KEYBOARD SHORT CUTS AND HOTKEYS

The following are some commonly used keyboard hot key combinations or shortcut keys in the Macbook,their functions and what they do.

SHORTCUT/ HOTKEY	FUNCTION
Command key + C	Copies a highlighted file or object
Command key + A	Highlights all files on a page or in a folder
Command key + V	Pastes copied item(s)
Command key + Z	To undo a change or effect
Command key + X	To cut a highlighted or selected item
Command key +O	Opens folders or files
Command key + F	To search for or find items in a

	folder
Command key + P	To print a screen or document or file on screen
Command + S	Saves an Open work or saves changes
Command key + H	Hide the window of the first app in open multiple windows
Option button+ Command key + H	Minimizes other opened window and leaves the main window open

Others include;

Control+Command key+F: For full-screen display

Command key +Tab: Opens the last used app in multiple app tabs **Shift+Command+(3,4 or 5):** Captures the screen image

Command key+W: Close the current tab from opened tabs(e.g in web apps or doc files).

Option Key+Command+W: Closes all open tabs within app.

Command key + Tab key:Runs through open apps in the opened order.
Command key + T:Opens a new tab.
esc key:Escapes or aborts an operation or undo a change or an effect.

The Mute button(🔇):removes audio or removes all sounds.

Volume button(🔊):For adjusting the volume of sound playing in both in the background and foreground.

Light adjustment keys(🔆)**and**(🔅):For increasing and decreasing screen brightness respectively.

Play/Pause button:To pause or play audio or video.

Next/Previous buttons⏩ **and** ⏪ : They are used for navigating playing audio or video collections.

DOCUMENT HOTKEYS

The following are hotkeys or keyboard key combinations for various operations when using a document application on a Macbook.

Control+A: Moves cursor to the start of the line.
Control+B: Moves one letter(character) in the backward direction.
Control+B: Moves one letter(character) in the forward direction.
Control+E: Moves cursor to the end of a line or paragraph.

Control+L: Positions cursor and make it visible.
Control+N: Move down one line.

Control+P: Moves cursor one line to the upside or paragraph.
Control-T: Exchanges characters at insertion points.
Control+H: Helps to delete the character or letter to the left.
Control+O: Inserts a new line
Control+D: Helps to delete the character or letter to the right.

Command+B: Makes selected text, bold or undo a selected bold text **Command+I:** Applies or undo italics effect on a text.
Command+K: Adds a web link or hyperlink to a selected text.

Command+U: Add or remove an underline effect to a selected text.
Command+T: Displays fonts.
Command+D: Displays desktop folders.
Control+Command+D: Displays

the properties of a selected word.
Command+Semicolon (;): Shows words with inaccurate spellings.

Fn key +Up Arrow: Move or Scroll one page up .
Fn key +Down Arrow: Move or Scroll one page down .
Fn key +Left Arrow(Home):Moves to the beginning of a document or page.
Fn key +Right Arrow(End): Moves cursor to the end of a document.

Command key+Left Curly Bracket [{]: Aligns selected texts to the left hand side.
Command key+Right Curly Bracket (}): Aligns selected texts to the right hand side.
Shift key+Command key +Vertical bar [|]:
Aligns selected text to the middle.
Option button+Command

key+F: Opens a search.
Option button+Command key +T: Displays the too bar.
Shift key+Command key+P: Displays document settings.
Shift key+Command key-S: Opens the 'save as' dialog box.

Shift key+ Command key + Minus(-): Reduces the font-size of selected texts or character.
Shift key+ Command key + Plus sign(+): Enhances the size of the selected letters or texts.
Shift key+Command key +Question mark (?): Displays the help menu.

Command key +Down Arrow: Takes the cursor to the end of the document.
Command+Left Arrow: Takes the cursor to the start of the line.

Command+Right Arrow: Takes the cursor to the start of the line.

Option key +Left Arrow: Takes the cursor to the start of the previous word.

Option key+Right Arrow: Takes the cursor to the end of the previous word.

Shift key +Command key+Left Arrow: Highlights the text from the cursor position to the left of the line.

Shift key+Command key +Right Arrow: Highlights the text from the cursor position to the right side of the line.

Shift+Up Arrow: Includes the line of texts above in the text highlighted texts.

Shift+Down Arrow: Includes the line(s) of texts below in the highlighted texts.

Shift+Left Arrow: Spread the text highlights over the text on the left hand side from the cursor position.

POWER KEYS
SHORT CUTS

These are keyboard shortcut keys or hotkey combinations that help to carry out operations such as shutting down the computer,putting the computer to sleep,restarting the computer,screen lock,etc.

Control key+Command key+Q: This combination causes the screen to be locked.To continue operating the computer it has to be unlocked thereafter.

Shift key+Command key+Q: To log out of a user account with a confirmation message.To log in again,the login credentials will have to be typed in to the login form on the login screen.

Power button: Turns the computer on or off when held for a couple of seconds.

Option key+Command key +Power button:
Puts the computer in sleep mode.

Option key+Command key +Media Eject ⏏:
Puts the computer in sleep mode.

Control key+Power button: Shows a dialog options to restart, sleep, or shut down the computer.

Control key+Command key +Power button:
Forces the computer to restart.

Control key+Command key +Media Eject key :
Prompts to save opened files,then quits any opened program and restarts the computer.

Control key+Option key +Command key+Power button:
Shuts down the computer

FINDER APP(EXPLORER) HOTKEYS

This hotkeys work on the finder app;
Command key+E: Displays
or ejects a selected key.
Command key+D: To another copy
or duplicate of a file or object.
Command key+I: Displays
info for a selected file.
Shift key+Command key+I: To open
the iCloud compartment or drive.
Shift key+Command key+K:
To display network area.
Option key+Command key+L:
Display the download folder.

Shift key+Command key+N:
To create a new folder.
Shift key+Command key+O:
To open document folder.

Shift key+Command key+U:
Display the utilities folder.

**Option key+Command key
+D:** Displays dock.

Option key+Command key+P:
Displays the path bar in Finder.

Option key+Command key+S:
Display the Sidebar in Finder.

Command key+Slash key(/):
Display the status bar in
Finder windows.
Command key+J: Displays

View options.

Command key+K: Opens server connection.

Command key+N: New window

Option key+Command key +N: To create a folder.

Command key+T: Displays the tab bar.

Option key +Command key+T: Displays the toolbar in finder.

Option key+Command key+V: To paste in the finder.

Shift key+Command key +G: Opens a go to Folder.

Shift key+Command key +H: Displays the home folder of a user account.

Shift key+Command key+P: Displays the Preview.

Shift key +Command key +R: To open Air Drop.

Command key+Right Bracket (]): Takes you to the next folder. **Command key + Up Arrow:** Displays the folder that houses the current sub-folder.

Command key+Control key+Up Arrow: Displays the folder that contains an opened sub-folder in a new window. **Command key +Down Arrow key:** Displays a selected element.

Command key+1: Displays objects as image icons. **Command key +2:** Displays files as a list. **Command key+3:** Displays objects or elements in columns. **Command**

key+4: Displays files in a gallery.

PHOTOS APPLICATION HOTKEYS

The following are important keyboard shortcut keys and hotkeys in using the photos application on a Macbook.

Command key+3:To crop a picture.
Command key+2: To apply filter to a picture.
Command key+1:To adjust a picture or image.
Command key+Option key+R:To rotate a picture clockwise Command key+R:Rotate a picture in the reverse direction. Command+E:To add effects to alter an original image.

Right Arrow key: Navigate to a new image in the forward direction.

Left Arrow key: Navigate to a previous picture or image in the backward direction.

Control key+M: Show the unaltered picture or the original.

Command key+Plus Sign (+): Zooms in an image or enhances.

Command key+Minus Sign(–): Zooms out an image.

Command key+Z : To undo the previous effect or change.

Shift key+Command key+Z: To redo the previous change or effect.

Command key+F: To search for a picture.

Space bar key: Pauses or plays images displaying in slideshow view mode.
Delete button: To delete a picture.

Command key+A: Selects all pictures.

Command key+N: To create an album.
Shift key+Command key+K: To create a Smart album.

Command key+L: Hide a selected picture.

Command key+I: To display image information.

Command key+D: To make a picture duplicate.
Command key+X: To cut an image.
Command key+C: To copy an image.
Command key+V: To paste a image.

Command key+W: To close

an open window.

Command key+M: Minimises open windows or tabs

Command key + H: This keeps the app hidden.

SAFARI WEB BROWSER KEYBOARD SHORTCUT & HOTKEYS

The safari is web browser for accessing and surfing the web or the internet.
Some hotkeys and keyboard shortcut keys include the following;

Command key+F: This opens a search dialogue box for the page.

Command key+P: Prints an open page.Or creates a PDF file.

Command key+C: This copies a highlighted item to the clipboard.

Command key+V: This pastes whatever is copied to the clipboard.

Shift key+Command key+(\) : Displays an overview of an opened tab.

Control key+Tab key: Move between open tabs.

Command key+Numbers(1,2,3...): To move between opened tabs.

Command key+W: To close an open tab.

Shift key+Command key+T: To re-open an already closed tab again.

Shift key+Command key +H: Navigate to Home

Command key+Plus Sign (+): Zoom in the page elements.

Command key+Minus Sign (-): Zoom out the page.

Control key+Command key +1: Displays bookmark bar.

Shift key+Command key +D: To add a page.

Shift key+Command key +T: Revisit a closed tab.

Shift key+Command key +R: This opens the reader.

Control key+Tab key: Takes one to the next tab.

Control key+Shift key+Tab key: Takes one to the previous tab

Space bar: Moves the page down.

Shift key+Space bar: Moves the page up.

FINAL NOTE

With all the above listed hotkeys and keyboard shortcut keys,operations around the Macbook computer become seamless and easy to carry out efficiently.
So practice,practice and practice some more! Until it becomes second nature to you.

DO MORE IN A SHORT TIME!

Please do leave a review on this book page on the Amazon store!

COMPUTER TECHNOLOGY MASTERY

Level up your knowledge and mastery of various technological operations via the use of the computer.

In a fast paced and advancing digital world where the use of computers have become a
common place and order of the day.
From free-lancing,online gigs, such as proof-reading & editing,coding,graphic design,video editing,
scripting,web design,spreadsheet & gaming as well as it's use in the corporate world .
Computer hot key mastery and coding skills are essential and near compulsory if we ever want to be efficient and move
speedily & efficiently working with PCs and our computers.
This series contain books to help you learn different computer technological operation s like web design,coding use of command prompt and keyboard mastery to help users level up their computer skill and use the
computer seamlessly.

Color Codes

The importance of Color cannot be Over-emphasized from the addition of color to fonts,
margins,backgrounds and Other web page elements to It's use graphic arts,paintings
and more.
This book COLOR CODES contains various colors & their codes to

help ease

the incorporation of colors in web design & other areas applicable.Thereby removing

the stress of having to refer to a given color.Color code is a manual for learners and

Professionals alike.

For Web designers & Developers,Soft ware & App developers,Graphic Artists and designers and so on.

Command Lines

Both basic and advanced operations on PCs,Computers
can be carried out using the command prompt Functionality.
A mastery of the command lines and codes helps to
simplify and make operations seamless around the Computer.
This book shows the various command lines and their functions.
This books looks at basic operations from turning off,restarting,logging off and
Aborting these processes to moderate operations such as partitioning &
disk/drive checks,connecting to computers ,task scheduling & reminder/alarm settings etc
Via thecommand prompt.

Html A-Z: All Operations In Html

HTML isthe language of the web, it is the frame-work of the web and website development.It is to a website what the skeleton is to the human body.

HTML A-Z is the ultimate book for html,as it simplifies,summarizes and explains all the integral aspects and components with practical examples,illustrations and application of HTML codes.

The book contains practical examples and illustrations to help learners and developers of all levels from beginner or rookie,students,intermediate to seasoned professionals to understand the language at a glance.

It delves in to the basics and core advanced topics from placing of text on a web page,to listing of items,addition of colors,forms;like text boxes,password box,drop-down lists,clickable buttons,Option or radio button,submit button,search ,to box query,addition of images to page,links, navigation page links,addition of clickable images to link objects,replacing links with graphic objects and other media files. Addition of downloadable contents such as;pdf,docx files,media files such as images,videos,animations,etc.

Computer Hot Key Mastery: Operate The Computer Seamlessly

In a fast advancing digital world where the use of computers have become a

common place and order of the day.

From free-lancing,online gigs, such as proof-reading & editing,coding,graphic design,video editing,

scripting,web design,spreadsheet & gaming as well as it's use in the corporate world .

Computer hot keys are essential and near compulsory if we ever want to be efficient and move

speedily & efficiently working with PCs and our computers.

This book lists some hot keys or keyboard shortcuts that facilitate and make the operationof the

computer seamless.

Core Css Simplified: Become Proficient In Css

This book contains invaluable and practical guide to the core of the Cascading Style Sheet(CSS) website or page development language.Lurking behind this cover are tools to style,beautify,trim,render and take a web page or site from a bare static HTML static page to a more beautiful & likable

web page and takes it a step closer to being an interactive and a more dynamic web page without the unnecessary details or grammars.The book illustrates,simplify and presents how to use CSS with practical examples and illustrations to make the reader(Beginner,novice or advanced) comprehend and be able to use CSS to build a fully functional stationary web page in no time. At the end of this book and upon completion,the reader will be able to use CSS to style a web page,add color codes,adjust page objects,images & attributes,as well as be able to use links,apply link attributes,position and align objects on a web page,adjust page attributes,elements,tweak,adjust or render web page attributes,add background image to web page,style & beautify link elements,join link pages & objects together and many more. A 100% mastery guaranteed.
PERFECT YOUR WEB CODING & DEVELOPMENT PROWESS !
WELCOME TO WEB DESIGN & DEVELOPMENT!

Color Shade: All Color Tints & Tones

There are various shades, tones,tints and hues to a given color,that can render it to appear or look different from its parent color,thereby making it relatively difficult to identify such a color.This book shows the various tone,tint, hue or shade of all known colors and their respective names to make for ease of identification,use and application even to the most color-blind. ... Know all the Colors & their variants!
Are you a color stylist,a Fashion designer,a tailor,a graphic artist,a painter,a Sketch artist,web designer or developer or in to any profession that requires the use of color and its application.Do you wish to know all the color variants,so that you can give your clients a wider range of options to chose from.Or are you a student or just a kid that is looking to learn or burn away some time doing that coloring or book painting.This book contains the various colors and their corresponding variants or modified forms,meaning,their appearance and their names to help you go beyond the basics and take your color mastery,combination and

application to a whole knew level.

www.ingramcontent.com/pod-product-compliance
Lightning Source LLC
Chambersburg PA
CBHW041155050326

40690CB00004B/573